LOST TRAMWAYS OF ENGLAND
LEEDS WEST

PETER WALLER

GRAFFEG

CONTENTS

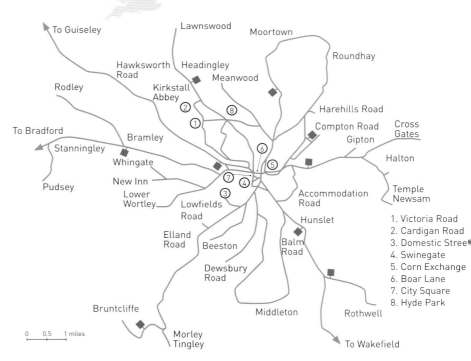

LEEDS WEST

To Guiseley
Lawnswood
Moortown
Roundhay
Hawksworth Road
Headingley
Meanwood
Rodley
Kirkstall Abbey
② ⑧
① Harehills Road
To Bradford
Compton Road
Cross Gates
Bramley
Gipton
Stanningley
⑥
Halton
Whingate
⑤
New Inn
⑦ ④
Lower Wortley
Temple Newsam
Pudsey
Lowfields Road
③
Accommodation Road
Elland Road
Hunslet
Beeston
Balm Road
Dewsbury Road
Bruntcliffe
Middleton
Rothwell
0   0.5   1 miles
Morley Tingley
To Wakefield

1. Victoria Road
2. Cardigan Road
3. Domestic Street
4. Swinegate
5. Corn Exchange
6. Boar Lane
7. City Square
8. Hyde Park

INTRODUCTION

Although there had been street tramways in Britain from the early 1860s in places like Birkenhead and London, it was not until the 1870 Tramways Act that a legislative framework was established for their construction and operation. The Act empowered local authorities to grant licences to companies to operate tramways for a 21-year period. The licensee could construct the tramway itself or the route could be constructed by the local authority and leased as part of the franchise to the operator. Initially, it was expected that private companies would always operate the tramways built; however, in 1883, Huddersfield Corporation in the West Riding of Yorkshire, having constructed a new steam tramway to serve the town, was unable to find a licensee willing to take on operation and so became the first municipal operator of trams within the British Isles.

The 1870 Act imposed a number of restrictions upon the tramway builder and operator; with the benefit of hindsight, it can be seen that these had a negative impact upon tramway development in the United Kingdom and undoubtedly represented one factor in the demise of the tramcar from the 1920s onwards. One of these clauses required the builder and operator of the tramway to maintain the public highway to a distance of 18 inches outside each running line; this effectively made the tramway owner responsible for the upkeep of the road surface on those streets where trams operated. At a time when the condition of the public highway was often poor, the well-built and well-maintained section over which the trams operated became a magnet for other road users. As road traffic increased, so trams – despite the fact that the road had been constructed to accommodate them – were increasingly perceived as a cause of road traffic delays.

The second weakness within the 1870 Act was the so-called 'scrap iron clause'; this permitted the licensor – usually the local authority – to take over the assets (such as the trams) owned by the licensee at asset value – including depreciation – rather than reflecting the value of the business. As a result, tramway licensees became increasingly unwilling to invest in their business as the licence period came towards its end. The Act permitted the termination of the licence after 21 years and every seven years thereafter. For company-owned operations this sword of Damocles meant that the threat of municipalisation was ever present and, even if never exercised, was sufficient to ensure that modernisation might never take place. The classic example here is the tramways of Bristol; operated throughout their career by a company but with the constant threat of take-over by Bristol Corporation, the system survived through until 1941 operating open-top and unvestibuled trams that would not have been out of place on the first electric tramways built at the end of the 19th century whereas other systems were operating state-of-the-art modern trams by World War II.

This volume is one of a series that cover the tramways of England and is one of two looking at the tramways of Leeds, covering the history of the early years of the tramways up to the outbreak of World War II and the routes that served the western half of the city. The second volume covers the World War II period and the post-war era and the routes to the east.

The early years

Leeds was to witness a relatively early tramway operation when, following the grant of the Leeds Tramways Order of 1871, William and Daniel Busby were granted powers to construct five routes. The first of these – from the centre to the Oak Inn in Headingley – opened on 16 September 1871. A second route – to the Cardigan Arms in Kirkstall – followed on 1 April 1872. The remaining three authorised routes – to the Crooked Billet at Hunslet, the Shoulder of Mutton on Marsh Lane and the Queens Arms in Chapeltown – were all opened by November 1874. By this date operation of the tramways had passed to the Leeds Tramway Co.

Under the new company two of the existing routes – to Headingley and Kirkstall – were extended; in addition, four new routes – to Meanwood, Wortley, Roundhay and Beckett Street – were all opened between 1878 and 1890. At its maximum extent the company's network stretched for about 14 route miles and was operated by up to 70 standard gauge horse trams.

On 25 October 1877 the company undertook its first experiments in the use of steam traction. These were to prove successful and regular steam-powered services were introduced from the early 1880s on a number of routes. The routes to Meanwood and Wortley – opened in 1878 and 1879 respectively – were constructed with heavier duty rail in order to facilitate the operation of steam trams and these commenced on the route to the Star, Wortley, on 7 June 1880. Steam services were introduced to the Headingley route in 1883 – these ceased in 1892 as a result of damage caused to the track – and, eventually, steam trams operated on a further five routes: to Kirkstall (in 1890), to Oakwood (from 1891), to Moortown (from 1894) and to Meanwood and to Hyde Park (both in 1898). Between 1880 and 1898 the company acquired 30 steam engines – all of which were manufactured locally (by either Kitson & Co Ltd or Thomas Green & Sons Ltd) – as well as hiring an additional two from Thomas Green.

The Roundhay company

The route from Sheepscar to Roundhay (Oakwood) was opened in February 1890; it was initially operated by horse trams but steam trams took over operation on 15 May 1891. The previous year the corporation had been approached by W. S. Graff Baker of the American Thomson Houston Co with a view to operating the new line with an alternative means of propulsion – electricity.

At the time, electric-powered transport was still relatively uncommon. There had been two lines in Ireland – the Giant's Causeway, Portrush & Bush Valley Railway & Tramway Co Ltd (first opened in 1883) and the Bessbrook & Newry (of 1885) – that were electric-powered largely using a third rail whilst the initial tramway in Blackpool – powered via a conduit – had also commenced operation in 1885. However, the new route in Leeds was to be the first street tramway in Britain to make use of overhead lines for the supply of electricity.

The new electric services were introduced on 11 November 1891 with a fleet of six single-deck trams all supplied by the New York-based manufacturer Stephenson Carriage & Wagon Co. A further two cars were acquired two years later, with an unpowered trailer car being acquired in 1896.

The corporation takes over

Following agreement over the value of its assets, the operations of the Leeds Tramways Co were taken over by the corporation on 2 February 1894. Initially the new owners supplemented the existing fleet by acquiring further horse cars but the intention was to electrify the existing system and to extend the network. Also acquired in February 1894 was the pioneering electric service to Roundhay; this was suspended on 31 July 1896 to facilitate modernisation and the new electric service – linking Kirkstall Abbey to Roundhay – commenced operation on 2 August 1897. Thereafter the conversion of the existing routes progressed, with the result that the last horse trams – along Whitehall Road – operated on 13 October 1901 and the last steam trams – to Bramley along Stanningley Road – followed on 1 April 1902. Electric services introduced during this period included Headingley (24 August 1899), Dewsbury Road (Cross Flatts Park; in two stages on 4 January 1900 and 15 June 1900), Meanwood (9 April 1900), Harehills Lane via Beckett Street (2 June 1900), Victoria Avenue (6 June 1900), Thwaite Gate (24 August 1900), Beeston (18 March 1901),

Hyde Park via Woodhouse Street (18 March 1901), Elland Road (19 April 1901), Cardigan Road via Burley Road and Victoria Road (both 3 August 1901), Whitehall Road (14 October 1901), Dixon Lane, Whingate and New Inn (all 10 January 1902), Stanningley (2 April 1902) and Easy Road (April 1902).

New routes and extensions were soon to follow. These included Roundhay via Moortown (in two stages on 18 May 1902 and 26 June 1902), Hyde Park via Belle Vue Road (3 September 1903), Compton Road via Beckett Street (6 April 1904), Elland Road to Churwell Dye Works and the branch to Domestic Street (both 21 May 1904), Victoria Avenue to Halton Dial (6 July 1904), Rodley (in two stages, from Bramley to Bramley Broad Lane on 14 April 1905 and thence to Rodley on 6 July 1906), Balm Road (1 June 1905), Dixon Lane to Lower Wortley (12 March 1907), Easy Road to South Accommodation Road (5 June 1908) and Headingley to West Park (11 September 1908). By 1908, the system employed some 282 electric tramcars.

Services beyond the boundaries

There were proposals by several companies to provide electric tramways beyond the city boundaries. The only connection to be completed by a company was the link through to Wakefield from Thwaite Gate that was opened by the Yorkshire (West Riding) Electric Tramways Co Ltd that commenced a service between Leeds and Wakefield on 15 August 1904. The company also constructed a branch to Rothwell that was largely operated by corporation cars from 1 June 1905.

Two other companies were to promote routes south-west from the existing terminus at Churwell Dye Works and west from Kirkstall Abbey. When neither of these completed the proposed lines, they were constructed with Leeds undertaking the operation. The first to be extended was the route to Kirkstall Abbey; the westward extension opened in three stages: Kirkstall Abbey to Horsforth (16 May 1906), Horsforth to Yeadon (26 May 1909) and Yeadon to Guiseley (Oxford Road) on 1 July 1909.

The track south-west of the terminus at Churwell Dye Works was leased to the corporation by Morley Corporation and also opened in three stages: Churwell Dye Works to Morley (5 July 1911), Morley to Tingley Mill (21 October 1911) and Morley to Bruntcliffe (1 January 1912).

There was also one further extension outside the then city boundaries: this was the extension from Stanningley to Pudsey which opened on 5 June 1908.

The Bradford through service

At Stanningley the system met the tramways operated by Bradford Corporation. Unlike Leeds, which had adopted the standard gauge, the latter had chosen to use the narrow gauge of 4ft 0in. Theoretically, therefore, the 8½in difference in gauge ought to have precluded the operation of through tramway services; however, with the introduction of tapered tracks providing a connection between the two systems and with a number of modified trams designed to permit operation on both gauges, a through service was introduced on 22 April 1907. Although suspended between 26 May 1907 and 23 September 1907 and again between 11 May 1908 and 8 June 1909, the service was to survive through until 25 March 1918.

The trolleybus years

In June 1911, Leeds – alongside Bradford – was to introduce the first regular trolleybus services in Britain. The first Leeds service ran alongside the existing tram route from City Square along Whitehall Street before running beyond the existing terminus to reach New Farnley. This was followed by two routes that connected into the existing tram terminus at Guiseley: the routes to Burley and to Otley both opened in late 1915. Unlike Bradford, however, where the trolleybus was destined to prosper (and survived until final abandonment in March 1972), the trolleybus in Leeds was not to survive long after the appointment of William Chamberlain as general manager in January 1925. He was not a trolleybus supporter and the New Farnley route ceased in 1926 and the last Leeds trolleybuses operated in July 1928, contemporaneously with Chamberlain's departure. He and his predecessors – particularly John Baillie Hamilton (who held the role from 1902 until 1925) – oversaw the continued development of the tramway system.

Further expansion

Following the opening of the New Farnley trolleybus route, the next few years witnessed the continued expansion of the tramway network. There was to be one extension completed prior to the outbreak of World War I; this was the line from West Park to Lawnswood which was opened on 18 April 1913.

There were to be five extensions completed during World War I. The first of these saw a short extension to the existing Guiseley route – from Oxford Road to the White Cross (were it connected later in the year with the new trolleybus routes) – on 8 March 1915. The second – on 30 April 1915 – saw the extension from Halton Dial to Halton. This was followed on 14 August 1915 by the extension of the Dewsbury Road route from Cross Flatts Park to Old Lane (Tommy Wass's). Two extensions followed in 1916: these were from Halton Dial to Killingbeck on 20 May and the direct route to Compton Road, via Nipper Lane, on 5 December.

The next significant event was in fact the first abandonment to affect the system. The track on the Whitehall Street route – which ran in parallel to the New Farnley trolleybus service – was, by

1920, in an increasingly poor condition; given the circumstances, approval for the abandonment of the tram service was given in early 1921 and it was converted on 15 June 1922.

Elsewhere, however, there were proposals for the development of new routes; as elsewhere in Britain, vast new housing estates were being constructed in the suburbs as a means of reducing the level of slum accommodation. There was a need for these estates to be served by public transport and, in Leeds, a number of these estates were to be served by tram.

Between the two world wars, a number of extensions were completed. The first of these – in two stages (on 18 April 1924 and 21 April 1924) – saw the new route off the Halton service to Temple Newsam opened. Although the first section of this was along Temple Newsam Road, the terminus in the park was reached via a reserved track section. The next – on 23 September 1924 – saw the Killingbeck service extended to Cross Gates. On 31 August 1925 a siding was opened on Lowfields Road, off the Elland Road route; this served two purposes: firstly, it permitted the storage of a number

of trams to operate as football specials after matches held at Elland Road and, secondly, it allowed access into the adjacent yard.

The same year – on 10 November – saw the opening of the first stage of the Middleton route off the Dewsbury Road route; the new route was extended through to Lingwell Road on 26 November 1927. Apart from the initial short section along Moor Road, this route was entirely on reserved track through Middleton Woods or along a central reservation on Middleton Park Road.

The final extension to the system prior to World War II came with the opening of the route to Gipton on 11 September 1936. There were further plans for further extensions in the east, most notably to serve the Seacroft estate, but these were never undertaken.

Other improvements

Many of the routes opened during the inter-war years were completed using sections of segregated track. In the years after 1918, as the level of other transport increased, so there was an increased awareness that, without remedial action, trams could cause congestion and issues of road safety.

One means of segregating the trams from other traffic was through the construction of reserved track sections and, from the early 1920s, the corporation undertook a considerable amount of work to achieve this. Amongst the sections of route that were transferred to reserved track were Harehills to Oakwood (21 May 1922), Oakwood to Roundhay (29 July 1923), Armley Park to Cockshott Lane (18 January 1931), Harehills Lane to Halton Dial (24 April 1932), Halton Dial to Killingbeck (8 May 1933), Selby Road (8 November 1936), West Park to Lawnswood (20 August 1938) and Cockshott Lane to Green Hill Mount (1939).

In addition to this work, a number of sections of line that had been constructed as single track with passing loops – such as part of the Lawnswood route along Otley Road and a short section along Halton Hill – were to be doubled during the 1930s; this work was continued during World War II.

During the 1930s, again in order to improve efficiency (and ease of overhead maintenance),

the overhead was gradually modified to permit the use of bow collectors in place of the traditional trolleypoles.

A change of policy

The first significant abandonment – other than the Whitehall Street route in the early 1920s – occurred as a result of the decision of the Yorkshire (West Riding) Tramways Co Ltd to convert its network to bus operation. On 31 May 1932 the company-operated through service to Wakefield and the corporation service (over company track beyond Thwaite Gate) to Rothwell – route 25 – were replaced by buses. As a result, the Hunslet route operated thereafter to a terminus at Thwaite Gate.

In terms of the Leeds network, much more significant was a decision made in 1932 – in order to improve the finances of the operator – that all routes beyond the city boundary as well as those constructed as primarily single track with passing loops were to be abandoned. The execution of the policy was to start in 1934 when, on 30 January, route 6 (Hyde Park via Cambridge Road and Woodhouse Street) was converted and route 7 was cut back from Hyde Park to Abyssinia Road; this route then operated as effectively a peak hour shuttle until the section from Park Lane to Abyssinia Road was converted on 5 June 1934.

The long semi-rural route beyond Hawskworth Road to Guiseley was the next casualty; this was abandoned 16 October 1934. This was followed on 22 January 1935 with the closure of the routes via Morley to Tingley and Bruntcliffe beyond the Churwell Dye Works; the route was further cut back from the dye works to the greyhound stadium on 8 January 1938. The last of the routes outside the city boundary – from Stanningley to Pudsey – was converted on 3 December 1938.

During this period a number of predominantly single track sections within the city itself also succumbed. Route 20, the service from York Road to South Accommodation Road, was converted on 25 February 1936, this was followed on 1 May 1937 by the conversion of the section of route 27 along Burley Road and the southern section of Cardigan Road. The Domestic Street service – route 29 – was the next to go, on 4 December 1937 with the last of the city pre-war closures – the service to Rodley (route 15) – taking place on 17 May 1938.

When war broke out in September 1939, the Leeds tramway network was in a strong position. The fleet had undergone considerable modernisation from the mid-1920s – some 300 trams had been built between 1925 and 1935, including the 17 stylish modern-looking 'Middleton Bogie' cars delivered between 1933 and 1935, whilst, in a portent for the future, three 1930-built trams had been acquired second-hand from the London Passenger Transport Board – whilst the system served had benefited from considerable investment in new routes and improvements to existing services.

A note on the photographs

The majority of the illustrations in this book have been drawn from the collection of the Online Transport Archive, a UK-registered charity that was set up to accommodate collections put together by transport enthusiasts who wished to see their precious images secured for the long-term. Further information about the archive can be found at: www.onlinetransportarchive.org or email secretary@onlinetransportarchive.org

THE EARLY YEARS

Following the Leeds Tramways Order
of 1871, the first horse trams in the
city commenced operation from the
centre to The Oak at Headingley
on 16 September 1871. Initially the
trams were operated by Daniel and
William Busby but the powers were
transferred to the Leeds Tramways
Co, the company that operated all
of the tramways in the city until the
corporation acquired its assets. The
corporation took over operation of the
company's routes on 2 February 1894.
Pictured about 1890, this view records
one of the company's Starbuck-built
double-deck horse trams in Briggate.

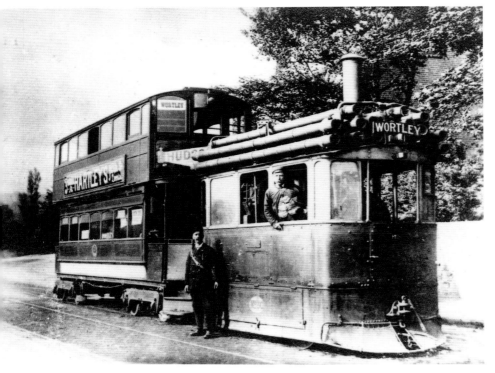

The first steam trams operated in Leeds, courtesy of the Leeds Tramways Co, on 17 June 1880 on the route to Wortley. Eventually the company was to own 30 tram engines – Nos 1-30 – plus two more hired from the locally based Thomas Green & Sons Ltd. No 30 – pictured here with a double-deck trailer – was one of two new engines, the last to be acquired, bought from Thomas Green & Sons in 1897. The final steam trams operated in Leeds on 1 April 1902. The Tong Road routes, including the branches to Whingate and New Inn, were electrified on 10 January 1902.

Although Leeds Corporation constructed the Sheepscar to Roundhay service, the primary leasee of tramway services in the city – the Leeds Tramway Co – were unwilling to take on the new route and so a new operator – the US-based Thomson-Houston Co – eventually took it on. Although initially horse and then steam operated briefly from February 1890 when originally opened (leased to W. S. Graff Baker), on 29 October 1891 electric tramcars were introduced. These were the first street trams in Britain to be powered by overhead electricity. Six single-deck trams were supplied by the New York-based Stephenson Carriage & Wagon Co for the new service; these were supplemented by three trailers supplied in 1893 and 1896. This pioneering service ceased on 31 October 1896, following the corporation's take-over, and were restored in July and August 1897.

Of the 10 trams supplied to the Roundhay Electric Tramways, a total of seven were used by the corporation as trailer cars.

Electric trams started to operate from Briggate to Kirkstall Abbey on 2 August 1897. This was extended to Horsforth (Calverley Lane) on 16 May 1906. From there it reached Yeadon (Green Lane) on 26 May 1909 and Guiseley (Oxford Road) on 1 July 1909; the final extension saw it reach Guiseley (White Cross) on 8 March 1915. This view sees

No 78 – one of a batch of 50 open-top four-wheel cars supplied by Brush in 1902 on Peckham 10 Cantilever four-wheel trucks that were converted to open-balcony top-covered cars between 1903 and 1906 – in Guiseley. The route was popular with walkers as the terminus gave easy access into Wharfedale. However, by the early

1930s the corporation's policy was to see the conversion of routes outside the city boundary – such as that to Guiseley – and those with a significant element of single track converted to bus operation so, on 16 October 1934 the Guiseley route was converted beyond the borough boundary at Hawksworth Road.

Another pre-World War II conversion was the Rodley route. This had originally opened in two stages: from Bramley Town End to Bramley Broad Lane on 14 April 1905 and thence to a new terminus at Bagley Lane, Rodley, on 6 July 1906. Although much of the second section was double track, the line opened in 1905 was predominantly single track with passing places. This view of No 153 – one of 50 open-top uncanopied trams, Nos 133-82, supplied by Brush on Peckham Cantilever four-wheel trucks in 1899 – sees the tram heading outbound towards Rodley along Town Street. The section of this route along Whitecote Hill, with its severe gradient, resulted in this route requiring operation by trams fitted with mechanical track brakes for safety. The only other route in Leeds that required this type of brake was the 14 to Pudsey for the section along Richardshaw Lane. The Rodley route was converted to bus operation on 17 May 1938.

The long route via Morley to either Bruntcliffe or Tingley was extended from the borough boundary at Churwell Dye Works to Morley Town Hall on 5 July 1911; two further extensions – to Tingley Mill and Brunctliffe – opened on 21 October 1911 and 1 January 1912 respectively. The decision to abandon services beyond the borough boundary saw route 24 cut back to the dye works on 22 January 1935, the section between the greyhound stadium and the dye works was abandoned on 8 January 1938. This view – taken at the Bruntcliffe terminus – records No 355 on the final day of the section. This was one of the last batch of open-balcony trams acquired by the corporation. Built at Kirkstall Road Works in March 1922, it was fitted with a Hurst Nelson-supplied 21E four-wheel truck but, by the date of this photograph, had been re-equipped with a Peckham P22. In October 1936 the car was rebuilt as fully enclosed and, as such, remained in service until July 1949. Note the crew wrapped up against the cold. With no heating, the platforms were damp and draughty.

The section from Stanningley to Pudsey opened on 5 June 1908, with the new terminus situated in front of the Commercial Hotel at the west end of Chapeltown at its junction with Uppermore and Greenside. One of the early production batch of 'Horsfield' cars – No 157, still equipped with a trolleypole – is pictured at the terminus towards the end of the route's operation by tram. The section from Stanningley was largely single track with passing loops and, in line with the corporation's policy of abandoning such sections, was converted to bus operation on 3 December 1938. The limit was now Cohen's Foundry Stanningley which was served in peak hours only, with the all-day service terminating at Half Mile Lane. The Pudsey route was the last service in Leeds to operate using trolleypoles.

Viewed looking towards the north, 'Chamberlain' No 427 has just come down Park Row and is picking up passengers in City Square prior to turning left into Boar Lane with a service towards Moortown on route 2. This angle gives a good view of the car's pivotal track; by this date this would have been locked in position. The tracks heading off to the left are those along Infirmary Street. Before the pre-war conversions, Infirmary Street was used by cars on routes 7 (to Hyde Park) and 27 (to Cardigan Road via Burley Road) but when recorded here was used solely by trams accessing St Paul's Street to head along Kirkstall Road. This view is virtually unrecognisable today. The building accommodating the branch of Barclays Bank on the left was demolished in 1967 (and its successor, the Norwich Union Building, has

also been redeveloped). The building was built originally for Standard Life Assurance in 1901 but was used latterly by Norwich Union. The neo-Gothic building across Park Row from the bank has also disappeared. However, the Mill Hill Chapel, which is on the right of the view and partially hidden by the tram, is still extant. This Grade II* listed Unitarian Chapel was designed by Henry Bowman and Joseph Crowther and was completed in 1848.

One of the earliest of the production 'Horsfield' cars – No 156 – is seen at the western end of Boar Lane with an outbound service to Moortown via Chapeltown. The tram is about to turn left into Briggate at the start of its outbound journey. Built by Brush and fitted with a Peckham P35 truck, No

156 entered service during March 1931; it was ultimately to be one of the type that saw service on the system's final day in November 1959. The section of route to Moortown via Chapeltown, part of the Roundhay loop, was converted to bus operation on 28 September 1957. This view of Boar Lane is still similar

today – although lacking the trams – as the parade of shops on the corner of Briggate and Boar Lane remains extant as does the neo-classical Holy Trinity Church (designed by William Etty of York and completed in 1727); the only casualty is the C&A store which has been redeveloped.

Looking in pristine condition, one of the three ex-London Transport 'HR/s' class cars acquired in the late 1930s – No 277 – is pictured turning from City Square into Boar Lane with a service on route 2 towards Roundhay via Chapeltown Road. Leeds had hoped to acquire more of these trams but the delayed conversion programme in London, as a result of the war, prevented this. The circular building in the background was, at the time, a bank; it was originally designed by W. W. Gwyther for the Yorkshire District Bank and completed in 1899. The building – now in use as a bar – is still extant. The tracks heading to the right of the bank head down Bishopgate Street and under the railway, providing the westernmost connection between the northern and southern sections of the network.

Two trams – 'Feltham' No 558
and 'Chamberlain' No 111 – head
eastbound through City Square on
services to Halton and Cross Gates
respectively. Although undated, the
view must have been taken between
December 1951, when No 558 entered
service, and March 1956, when No
111 was withdrawn. The backdrop is
dominated by the old General Post
Office; this was designed by Sir Henry
Tanner and opened in 1896. Still extant,
the building is now listed Grade II.
To the left can be seen the Majestic
Cinema; built to the designs of Pascal
J. Steinlet and Joseph C. Maxwell,
the building, situated on the corner of
Wellington Street and Quebec Street,
opened on 5 June 1922. Closed as a
cinema in 1969, it functioned as a bingo
hall until 1996. The listed but vacant
building was seriously damaged by fire
in September 2014. Work to convert it
into offices commenced in 2018 and,
in April 2019, it was announced that
Channel 4 was to base its relocated
headquarters in the building.

With the Prince of Wales pub in the background, 'Middleton' bogie No 257 picks up passengers on Bishopgate Street prior to heading down Swinegate, under the railway bridge obscured by the two trams, before heading out along Hunslet Road with a service on the Middleton circle. Two batches of 'Middleton' bogies were acquired; the first nine, Nos 255-63, were supplied by Brush during 1933 and 1935 whilst a further eight, Nos 264-71, were built by English Electric in 1935. All were equipped with Maley & Taunton equal-wheel bogies. Although undated, the photograph must post-date November 1953, as that was when No 257 first emerged in a new red livery but without lining out. All bar one of the 'Middleton Bogies' were withdrawn in 1956; the final example succumbed the following year. Although the trams are long gone from this view, the pub in the background – now renamed the Moot Hall Arms – is still extant, as are the railway arches on the right; the station above, however, has been considerably rebuilt (on several occasions) since the early 1950s.

Viewed looking towards the east on 12 September 1954, 'Feltham' No 529 heads outbound along Wellington Street with a service on route 16 towards New Inn. Four tram routes historically used this section: the 14 to Stanningley and Pudsey, the 15 towards Rodley, the 16 to either New Inn or Whingate and the 19 towards Lower Wortley. However, by the date of the photograph, there were only two services remaining; these were to Whingate (which had become route 15 on 1 October 1950) and to New Inn. These two services were converted to bus operation on 21 July 1956. No 529 had been London Transport No 2116 and entered service in the West Riding during April 1951. It was one of the type that survived through until final closure.

The unique wartime replacement four-wheel car No 275 is seen on 11 June 1950 heading eastwards along Wellington Street with a service on route 14. Although the tram shows Half Mile Lane as its destination, the tram is actually heading towards the city centre – the driver having the blind ready for the next outbound trip. The tram is passing the crossover at the junction with Little King Street. Although the West Riding Hotel, on the extreme right of the photograph, still exists, the prominent building occupied by Firth, Ray & Prosser, decorators' merchants, is no more; the site is now occupied by a modern – pastiche – office block called Wellington House that is occupied by the West Yorkshire Combined Authority.

With the background dominated by Leeds City railway station, the more orthodox of the two railcoaches built by C. H. Roe Ltd in 1953 – No 601 – is seen about to turn left into Neville Street prior to heading outbound with a service towards Hunslet. Fitted with bogies supplied by the Electro-Mechanical Brake Co Ltd, No 601 could accommodate 34 seated and 36 standing passengers. Leeds New station – jointly promoted by the London & North Western and North Eastern railways – first opened in 1869; in 1938, it was merged with Wellington station and the combined station was named Leeds City. The first major rebuilding of City station took place in the mid-1960s, when Central station was closed, and the station was again expanded and rebuilt between 1999 and 2002.

Historically, two routes used Vicar Lane: these were the 6 to Hyde Park via Cambridge Road and Woodhouse Street and the 23 to Meanwood. On 7 June 1951, one of the ex-Manchester cars – No 286 – is seen heading north with an outbound service to Meanwood. In the years during and after the war, Leeds acquired a significant number of second-hand trams both to replace older cars and also to meet post-war demand. The Hyde Park service was a relatively early casualty, being cut back to a spur on Cambridge Road on 30 January 1934; this was to last until 5 June 1934, when the Cambridge Road service was converted. The route number 6 was then reallocated to the Meanwood service (from 8 January 1938) and it is therefore this route number that No 286 displays. The Meanwood service was converted to bus operation on 25 June 1955.

In the background, at the junction of Eastgate and Vicar Lane, is the County Hotel; this was originally called the Tate Temperance & Commercial Hotel and the building – now cleaned – is still extant, albeit no longer a hotel.

No 104 was destroyed as a result of enemy action; the likelihood of being able to replace the tram with a new tram was remote but the wartime traffic demands meant that a replacement car became essential. As a result work, commenced on the construction of an 'Austerity' car, No 104. This utilised the electrical equipment salvaged from the remains of the destroyed tram as well as a second-hand Peckham P35 truck (acquired from the Llandudno & Colwyn Bay Electric Railway) with a body constructed in Kirkstall Road Works. The new tram entered service in 1943 and was renumbered 275 in 1948. When seen here it still retained its original two-line destination display, which was modified to show a single line in August 1951. No 275 was withdrawn in September 1957 and scrapped the following month.

There was a complex junction outside the Corn Exchange, along with loops for cars that used the location as their city centre terminus. One of the services that terminated at the Corn Exchange was route 14 which, by the date of this photograph (4 June 1951), operated only as far as Half Mile Lane in Stanningley. Pictured at the terminus is No 275; this was a unique car constructed during World War II. On 3 July 1942 'Chamberlain' car

As pedestrians cross the road to gain access to the central loading refuges on Briggate, the photographer has taken advantage of the lack of traffic to record a 'Horsfield' car on route 3. The majority of the buildings in this view have been replaced – the Imperial Hotel, on the right, for example, was demolished in 1961 to permit the construction of a replacement shop for Burton Tailoring – the building with the cupola at the junction of Briggate with Duncan Street, which is now occupied by the Yorkshire Building Society, remains as a point of reference. The cast-iron barriers for the shelters, which replaced earlier concrete barriers, were installed in 1930 following an accident in June the previous year when a lady had been fatally crushed between the barriers and a tram heading to Lawnswood.

Pictured at the junction of New Briggate and Vicar Lane on 9 June 1951, 'Horsfield' No 216 is about to take the former with an inbound service on route 3. This tram, new in September 1931, was to survive in service until March 1959.

Historically, Vicar Lane was used by routes 6 and 23 (renumbered 6 in 1938 following conversion of the Hyde Park route) to Hyde Park and Meanwood respectively. This view is unrecognisable today, with the junction now forming part of the intersection with the A64(M) New York Road.

Pictured standing on the loop in front of the Corn Exchange on 10 June 1950 is 'Horsfield' No 228 awaiting departure with a service on route 14 to Half Mile Lane. Inbound cars headed up New Market Street before turning into the loop, then heading outbound via Call Lane and Duncan Street. In the background, the two buildings on the junction of Kirkgate and New Market Street are still extant, although the oyster bar owned by Thomas Haye is no more (although a more modern oyster bar – Hayes – can now be found in Kirkgate Market). Whilst the tram loop is also now long gone, modern and extended bus shelters along both Call Lane and New Market Street emphasise that this is still an important public transport interchange.

Arguably the most modern first-generation tramcar constructed in Britain was Leeds No 602. One of the three single-deck trams constructed as part of the programme for the possible construction of tram subways in the city centre, the body of No 602 was completed in 1953 by the locally based Charles H. Roe and equipped with PCC-style trucks supplied by Maley & Taunton and VAMBAC electrical equipment manufactured by Crompton-Parkinson. No 602 – along with more conventional sister car No 601 – were delivered in a non-standard purple livery to mark the coronation of HM Queen Elizabeth II. In April 1954, No 602 is shown to good effect on the loop, installed in 1931, from Kirkgate into New York Street that was the city terminus of route 22 to Temple Newsam. The third single-deck car – No 600 – was rebuilt from ex-Sunderland No 85.

The three single-deck cars were used initially on a number of services but eventually eked out their existence on the Hunslet service. All were withdrawn in September 1957 with all three passing into preservation. Whilst No 600 and 602 now form part of the National Tramway Museum's collection, No 601 was less fortunate. Stored on the Middleton Railway, it suffered severe damage from vandalism and was subsequently scrapped. Although no longer a bank, the building then occupied by the Yorkshire Penny Bank (designed by Smith and Tweedale and completed in 1899) is still extant. The buildings along the north side of New York Street are also still present, although that towards the north-east has been considerably modified.

Pictured turning from New Market Street into Duncan Street with a service on route 5 towards Beeston is 'Horsfield' No 170. Visible behind the tram is the Star & Garter public house whilst on the corner of Call Lane, across the road from the Corn Exchange, is the impressive building then occupied by W. H. Smith. Whilst the buildings at the junction with Duncan Street are still extant – albeit the Star & Garter is no longer a pub (having closed in the 1970s) and is boarded up – the erstwhile W. H. Smith building has been redeveloped and Cloth Hall Street is now pedestrianised.

The Beeston service – which was linked in later years with Meanwood (until 25 June 1955) and Harehills – was finally converted to bus operation on 19 November 1955 by which time it terminated on Vicar Lane. No 170 was to last slightly longer, being withdrawn in June 1959.

With the premises of J. Gillinson, Gibbon & Demaine Ltd – wholesale drapers of 1-13 New York Street – in the background, 'Feltham' No 533 is pictured on Call Lane heading inbound; the driver has prepared the blind for the outbound journey back towards Cross Gates. The track along Call Lane was modified in 1942 whilst the single track heading in from the left is the loop in front of the Corn Exchange used by cars on routes 12, 14, 15 and 25 that terminated there. The awning shows part again of the Thomas Haye's Oyster Bar. The visible buildings are still extant, although 1-13 New York Street has been re-roofed with the loss of the curious little spire.

Recorded at the terminus of the 'Beeston' route is 'Horsfield' No 245. The 100 'Horsfield' trams, built by Brush during 1931 and 1932 on Peckham P35 trucks, were the last traditional four-wheel trams delivered new to the corporation. Although the type was one that, along with the ex-London Transport 'Felthams', were to survive in significant numbers through to the system's closure, No 245 was destined to be the first 'Horsfield' to be withdrawn from service – in late March 1954 – although it was not scrapped until July 1956. The terminus at Beeston was cut back by a short distance – 100 yards – in 1941. During the early 1950s the number of journeys that operated to Beeston were reduced and final conversion of the route occurred on 19 November 1955.

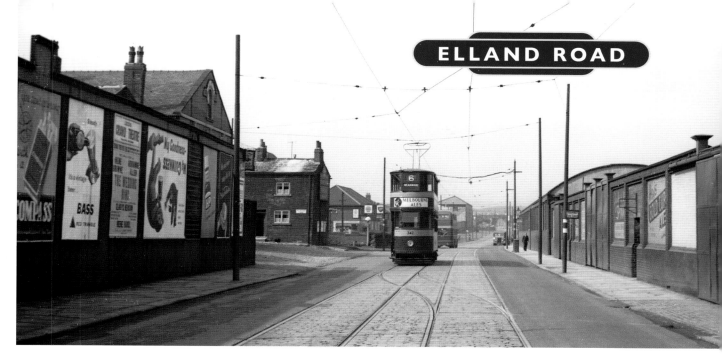

'Horsfield' No 242 awaits departure from the Elland Road terminus alongside the greyhound stadium. The Elland Road service had, originally, been part of a longer route that had operated through to Morley and Bruntcliffe. The route had, however, been cut back to the city boundary at Churwell Dye Road Works on 22 January 1935 and was further curtailed, to the terminus illustrated here, on 8 January 1938. The short section from the greyhound stadium to Leeds United's football ground was abandoned during 1954. The greyhound stadium was originally opened on 16 July 1927; it was to last just over 50 years before its closure on 15 March 1982. Subsequently demolished, the site is now occupied by a police headquarters. No 242 was finally to be withdrawn during March 1958.

Heading along Low Fields Road was a single-track siding that provided access to a permanent way yard and accommodation for trams dealing with the crowds after football matches at the adjacent Elland Road ground of Leeds United; the siding, which could accommodate 70 cars when necessary, was opened on 31 August 1925 and it was along this section that many Leeds trams made their final journey as they headed to Low Fields Road Yard for scrapping. Pictured on the siding outside the yard is stores car No 2. This had originally been open-balcony No 73 – renumbered 73A after 1926 – which had been built by Brush and delivered in 1904. Initially fitted with a Brush-built AA four-wheel truck it was later equipped with a Brill 21E. Converted into a works car in 1937, it was last used in late 1956 when it was transferred to Swinegate for storage. It was transferred to Torre Road Depot yard in July 1957 (again for storage), before returning to Swinegate for scrapping in October 1959.

Having diverged from the Whingate and New Inn routes to head along Oldfield Lane, the Lower Wortley terminus of route 19 was in front of the William IV public house on Lower Road. The route, after turning off Wellington Road, was predominantly single track with passing loops and was, therefore, a relatively early post-war conversion as the pre-war policy of abandoning this type of tramway was completed. Route 19 was converted to bus operation on 23 August 1946 – one of two routes (the other being the 11, serving Beckett Lane) converted that day; these were the first post-war conversions in the city. Here 'Chamberlain' No 14 is seen approaching the loop at the route's terminus.

One of the ex-MET 'Felthams' – No 544 – stands at the terminus at New Inn, Wortley. This had been LPTB No 2090 and entered service in the West Riding in July 1951. It was, however, destined for a relatively short life in Leeds, being one of the first of the type to be withdrawn – in July 1956 – although it was not scrapped until September the following year. Like Whingate, services to New Inn were converted to bus operation on 21 July 1956. Cars showed 15 or 16 outbound but 18 or 20 returning to the city as they worked across town to Cross Gates (18) or Halton (20).

WHINGATE

The Whingate and New Inn routes both headed out of the city centre along Wellington Road and Tong Road before splitting at the junction of Tong Road and Whingate. Heading inbound from Whingate on a service on route 18 to Cross Gates is 'Feltham' No 588. When the London Passenger Transport Board was established in 1933, it acquired the 100 production 'Felthams' from two earlier operators: 54 from the Metropolitan Electric Tramways and 46 from the London United Tramways. The latter were to survive longer in London and thus, following the purchase, came later to Leeds. As a result, not all entered service. No 588, one of the ex-LUT cars, did so in Leeds in February 1952 and was withdrawn in October 1957.

Awaiting departure from Whingate with a service towards Cross Gates is 'Chamberlain' No 138. The Whingate route, from the existing route to New Inn at Whingate Junction, opened as a steam tram service on 30 March 1898. Electric tram services to both New Inn and Whingate commenced on 10 January 1902. The Whingate service was converted to bus operation on 21 July 1956. No 138 was new in April 1927; equipped with a replacement P35 truck in November 1947, the tram was finally withdrawn in March 1956.

The house on the extreme left, now extended and converted into a care home, is still extant and provides a useful reference point to the location of this former terminus on Hill Top Road.

Pictured at the then peak hour terminus outside the works of George Cohen Sons & Co Ltd of the Stanningley route on an enthusiasts' tour is 'Middleton Bogie' No 258. Note the twin headlamps; these were fitted to this type for operation through Middleton Woods. Note also the disconnected track in the background; this was the continuation of the route to Pudsey. The section between Half Mile Lane and Pudsey was converted to bus operation on 3 December 1938; thereafter service 14 operated as far as Half Mile Lane, being extended to the Cohen works only in peak hours. The last trams operated west of Half Mile Lane on 2 January 1953, with the remainder of the route being converted to bus operation on 3 October 1953. George Cohen Sons & Co Ltd has also disappeared, as have many of the buildings visible in this view; the one reference point is the two-storey building on the extreme right, which is still extant and now forms part of an Indian restaurant.

STANNINGLEY

Viewed looking east on Town Street, Stanningley, No 376 is seen heading inbound. This was one of 41 cars – Nos 370-410 – that were built at Kirkstall Road Works between 1923 and 1928 that were the first trams to be operated by the corporation that were fully enclosed from new. No 376 was completed in April 1924 and survived in service until June 1950. The route from the city centre to Stanningley opened in stages – operated by steam trams – between January 1900 and March 1902, with electric trams taking over operation on 2 April 1902. The extension from Stanningley to Pudsey, seen heading to the south in this view, opened on 5 June 1908. In the foreground can be seen the tracks that connected into the 4ft 0in gauge tramway operated by Bradford Corporation. Despite the difference in gauge, a through tram service – using tapered track and modified trucks that permitted the truck's gauge to change in transit over this section – was operated between 21 January 1907 and 25 March 1918 (with a couple of short interruptions in the early years). Leeds trams ceased to operate over this section of line, to the west of the Cohen works, on 3 December 1938. Bradford Corporation continued to serve Stanningley until 19 October 1942.

A short working for the Kirkstall Abbey route existed at Haddon Place; prior to World War II there had been a three-track layout but, at some date between 1942 and 1946 this was replaced by a siding located on reserved track at Woodside View (although the destination remained known as Haddon Place). Pictured on this siding in August 1951 is the second of the ex-London Transport 'Felthams' to enter service in Leeds, No 502, which had started its second career in October the previous year. It is pictured awaiting departure with a service on route 3 towards Harehills. The use of the loop at Haddon Place ceased on 7 March 1954, with all trams running through to Kirkstall Abbey until the final conversion of the route the following month. When it first entered service in Leeds, No 502 was painted in a non-standard red and green livery; this was not to last long, and when pictured here, the tram was in a predominantly all-red livery.

No 444 stands at the terminus at Kirkstall Abbey on 4 June 1951. This was the penultimate of the final batch of 'Chamberlain' cars – Nos 411-45 – that were delivered between 1926 and 1928. All were completed at Kirkstall Road Works and equipped with EMB Pivotal four-wheel trucks. No 444 was a relatively early casualty, being withdrawn in July 1952. The Kirkstall Abbey service was originally a short working on the much longer route beyond the borough boundary to Guiseley. This had been cut back to the boundary at Hawksworth Lane on 16 October 1934 and the section beyond Kirkstall Abbey was abandoned on 3 December 1949. The Kirkstall Abbey route was converted to bus operation on 3 April 1954. However, at the city end a short section along Kirkstall Road to the Works survived until 7 November 1957.

Following the abandonment of the long 10-mile semi-rural route through to Guiseley on 16 October 1934, the tram service along Kirkstall Road was cut back to Hawksworth Road. The section beyond Kirkstall Abbey to Hawksworth Road was destined to be one of the early post-war conversions, being abandoned on 3 December 1949 largely on financial grounds although this view taken the previous year of 'Convert' No 339 at Vesper Gate inbound with a service on route 3 towards Roundhay also illustrates how poor the condition of the track was prior to abandonment.

CARDIGAN ROAD

The route to Cardigan Road – up Burley Road and along Cardigan Road to its junction with St Michael's Road – was opened on 3 August 1901. At the same time, the existing steam tram route along Victoria Road to Cardigan Road was also electrified. Pictured at the Cardigan Road terminus is No 72; this was one of 25 cars built by Brush in 1904 that were the first trams operated in Leeds to be fitted with open-balcony top covers from new. In line with the corporation's pre-World War II policy of converting all routes with significant single-track sections to bus operation, the route along Burley Road and Cardigan Road, to its junction with Victoria Road, was converted to bus operation on 1 May 1937; thereafter the Cardigan Road service operated via Victoria Road and Woodhouse Lane until it too was converted to bus operation on 7 December 1947. As such, it was to be the last route in Leeds to have significant sections of single track with passing loops.

With the skyline dominated by the imposing Parkinson Building of Leeds University in the background, 'Horsfield' No 176 heads southbound past Trinity St David's Congregational Church (designed by G. F. Danby and completed in 1898) with a service that will pass through the city centre to head out onto the Moortown loop on 17 September 1954. New in May 1932, No 176 was one of the type that survived in service until the final closure of the Leeds system on 7 November 1959. When pictured here, the Parkinson Building was relatively new. Although work commenced on its construction, to a design by Thomas Lodge, in 1938, the outbreak of World War II resulted in building work being suspended and it was not until 9 November 1951 that the building was officially opened by the then Princess Royal, Mary, Countess of Harewood, who was the then university's chancellor.

One of the earliest post-war tram-to-bus conversions in Leeds was route 30, which operated from the city centre to the western end of Victoria Road at its junction with Cardigan Road. The section along Victoria Road itself, which was largely single track, was converted to bus operation on 8 December 1947. However, a short terminal stub, used by cars on route 27, was retained at the eastern end of Victoria Road and it is here that No 510, one of the ex-London Transport 'Feltham' cars, is pictured. The use of the surviving spur was relatively short-lived; it was replaced by a new crossover on the city side of Hyde Park junction on 15 August 1952. No 510 had originally been Metropolitan Electric Tramways No 328, becoming London Transport No 2074 on the creation of the London Passenger Transport Board in July 1933. Withdrawn in the metropolis in September 1950, it entered service in Leeds two months later. It was destined to survive until withdrawal in March 1959. Although lacking trams and with considerably more parked cars, Victoria Road is largely unchanged almost 70 years on.

In 1949 a new spur to accommodate trams that had previously terminated in front of Headingley depot was opened on St Chad's Road in order to reduce congestion on the main road. Here, with the depot building in the background, 'Horsfield' No 229 is seen departing with a service towards Roundhay in April 1954. No 229, originally new in October 1931, was to be withdrawn in March 1959 contemporaneously with the conversion of the routes to Moortown (via Harehills) and to Middleton (via both Moor Road and Belle Isle).

In April 1954 two of the earlier batches of 'Chamberlain' four-wheel cars are pictured at the Lawnswood terminus. On the right is No 71; this was one of the 75 – Nos 1-75 – built by Brush during 1926 and 1927 whilst, on the left, No 143 was one of the 75 – Nos 76-150 – built by English Electric during the same period. All were originally fitted with EMB Pivotal trucks but Nos 71 and 143 were amongst those fitted with replacement Peckham P35 trucks between 1944 and 1952. No 143 was to survive in service until July 1955 and No 71 last operated in February the following year. The Lawnswood service, which served some of the most prestigious addresses in the city, was finally converted to bus operation on 3 March 1956.

A further view of the terminus at Lawnswood in April 1954 sees the unique No 301. This tram had originally been built for the London County Council in 1932 and had been nicknamed 'Bluebird' as a result of its non-standard blue livery. Numbered 1 and fitted with a number of modern features including Electro-Mechanical Brake Co Ltd heavyweight bogies, the tram was intended as a prototype for a replacement fleet, but the creation of the London Passenger Transport Board in July 1933, which adopted a tram to trolleybus conversion programme, meant that no further examples were constructed. Withdrawn during London's post-war 'Operation Tramaway' – the plan that saw all London's surviving trams replaced by July 1952 – No 1 was sold to Leeds in 1951. A non-standard car, it was withdrawn in 1957 and subsequently preserved. At the time of writing it is undergoing a major restoration project at the National Tramway Museum.

With the Beckett Arms public house in the background, 'Horsfield' No 184 is seen at the terminus of the Meanwood route in April 1954. A total of 100 of this type of tram were built by Brush on Peckham P35 four-wheel trucks during 1931 and 1932. It was to survive in service until October 1958. The outbound Meanwood services carried route number 6 after 1938; returning cars carried the route numbers 5 if heading to Beeston or 8 if the ultimate destination was Elland Road. Tram services to Meanwood from Corn Exchange were converted to bus operation on 25 June 1955. The pub itself is now history; named after local benefactors, the building was demolished in 2007 and the site redeveloped for apartments.

CREDITS

Lost Tramways of England – Leeds West
Published in Great Britain in 2020
by Graffeg Limited.

Written by Peter Waller copyright © 2020.
Designed and produced by Graffeg Limited
copyright © 2020.

Graffeg Limited, 24 Stradey Park Business
Centre, Mwrwg Road, Llangennech, Llanelli,
Carmarthenshire, SA14 8YP, Wales, UK.
Tel: 01554 824000. www.graffeg.com.

Peter Waller is hereby identified as the
author of this work in accordance with
section 77 of the Copyrights, Designs and
Patents Act 1988.

A CIP Catalogue record for this book is
available from the British Library.

ISBN 9781913733506

1 2 3 4 5 6 7 8 9

Photo credits

© D. W. K. Jones Collection/Online Transport Archive: pages 13, 45. © J. Joyce Collection/ Online Transport Archive: pages 14, 15. © Barry Cross Collection/Online Transport Archive: pages 16, 17, 55. © W. Marsh via H. Heyworth/Barry Cross Collection/Online Transport Archive: page 19. © W. A. Camwell/ National Tramway Museum: page 20. © Peter Davey collection/Online Transport Archive: page 23. © F. E. J. Ward/Online Transport Archive: pages 24, 27. © J. H. Roberts/Online Transport Archive: pages 25, 48. © Keith Carter/Online Transport Archive: pages 28, 40, 41, 46, 47. © Julian Thompson/ Online Transport Archive: pages 29, 33, 34, 36, 52, 56. © John Meredith/Online Transport Archive: pages 30, 58. © C. Carter: page 31. © Phil Tatt/ Online Transport Archive on: pages 35, 39, 51, 59, 61, 62, 63. © Peter N. Williams/Online Transport Archive: page 37. © R. W. A. Jones/ Online Transport Archive: pages 42, 43, 44. © F. N. T. Lloyd-Jones/Online Transport Archive: page 49. © Geoffrey Morant Collection/Online Transport Archive: page 50. © R. B. Parr/ National Tramway Museum: page 53.

The photographs used in this book have come from a variety of sources. Wherever possible contributors have been identified although some images may have been used without credit or acknowledgement and if this is the case apologies are offered and full credit will be given in any future edition.

Cover: Wellington Street.

Back cover: Corn Exchange, Wortley, Kirkgate.